Game Over!

By Janette Arias

Illlustrated by Sergio Giovine

Dale Park was just about to pour cold milk on his *Brain Busters* cereal, when suddenly he noticed something shiny in the bowl. The morning sun reflected off of a golden wrapper.

Dale quickly ripped open the wrapper and found two free passes to Brain Busters Arcade.

"Cool!" Dale screamed.

Dale had never won anything before—except for a goldfish named Lucky. Dale won Lucky at a carnival by tossing a table tennis ball into a fish bowl.

Dale called his friend Flash. "Flash, you're not going to believe this, but I just won two free passes to Brain Busters!"

Dale waited to hear Flash's response. "Flash? Hello. . . did you hear me?"

Just then the doorbell rang. Dale's mother yelled, "Dale! Flash is here!"

Flash *was* the fastest kid in the 5th grade, but he lived three blocks away! Flash ran into the kitchen still wearing his pajamas. "What time do we leave?" Flash asked.

Several days later, the boys were at Brain Busters, the largest video arcade in the world. They had every kind of game you could imagine, and some you couldn't. The boys had VIG—Very Important Gamer—wristbands that gave them free access to all games.

After a few hours of video games, the boys noticed a man with thick glasses and hair pointing in all directions sitting next to a door. The sign on the door said *Danger Island*.

"Would you boys like to try a new game?" the inventor asked.

"How do we play the game?" Dale asked.

"Find and destroy the mad scientist's laboratory on Danger Island," he laughed.

"Sounds cool," Flash said.

As the boys entered the dark room, it suddenly started getting very hot. Then they heard the sounds of chirping insects, howling monkeys, and squawking birds. Gradually, the room became a thick jungle.

"Awesome!" the boys said at the same time.

    As the boys started walking through the jungle, they saw colorful birds and huge snakes hanging from trees.

    "This game is great!" Dale said. He swatted at a mosquito.

    "It seems so real," Flash said. He wiped sweat from his forehead.

    By midday they had walked many miles without finding the laboratory. They were hungry and tired.

    "I've got an idea," Flash said. "Why don't we pause this game and get something to eat?"

    "Where's the door?" Dale asked.

Now they were worried. They looked around for the game door. They ripped at plants as if they were curtains. They yelled for the inventor. Dale even clicked his heels together and said, "There's no place like home."

Then they spotted a jaguar slinking towards them.

"Nice kitty, kitty," Dale whispered.

"Run!" Flash yelled.

The boys ran as fast as they could. Flash kept slowing down for Dale. Eventually they found themselves at the edge of a cliff.

"Game over!" Dale yelled.

The jaguar crept closer. It was about to leap for their throats, when suddenly two arms reached out and pulled the boys out of the room. It was the inventor.

"Well, what do you think of my latest invention?" he asked.

"We were almost killed!" Dale shouted.

"I've never been so scared in my life!" Flash cried.

"I'm sorry. Is it too wild?" the inventor asked.

"Are you kidding?" Dale said. "That was the best game ever!"

"We're coming back!" Flash said.